THE MAD PUNTER STRIKES AGAIN

Peanuts® Parade Paperbacks

THE MAD PUNTER STRIKES AGAIN

WUMP

Cartoons from *Snoopy, Come Home* and *You Can't Win, Charlie Brown*

by Charles M. Schulz

Holt, Rinehart and Winston / New York

Published simultaneously in Canada by Holt, Rinehart
and Winston of Canada, Limited.

First published in this form in 1976.

Library of Congress Catalog Card Number: 76-8674

ISBN: 0-03-018126-7

Printed in the United States of America

10 9 8 7 6 5 4 3 2 1

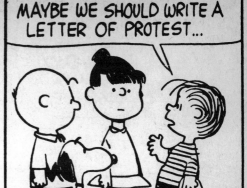

TO ME, THE UGLIEST SIGHT IN THE WORLD IS AN EMPTY DOG DISH!

I GET THE HINT!

I BET I'D MAKE A PRETTY GOOD HOOD ORNAMENT!

MY GLASSES! I CAN'T FIND MY NEW GLASSES!

THE OPHTHALMOLOGIST WILL KILL ME IF I'VE LOST MY NEW GLASSES!

DON'T WORRY...SOMEBODY WILL FIND THEM, AND BRING THEM BACK TO YOU...

SEE? WHAT DID I TELL YOU?

I JUST WANT YOU TO KNOW THAT THREE HUNDRED AND FIFTY MILLION DOLLARS A YEAR IS SPENT ON DOG FOOD!

I WONDER IF THAT INCLUDES TIPS!

MY WHOLE TEAM IS DESERTING ME

ONE BY ONE THEY'VE BEEN TURNING IN THEIR CAPS..

I WONDER WHO'LL BE NEXT...

⁂ SIGH ⁂

SEE WHAT YOU STARTED?

My home is always open to those who enjoy discussion groups!

Sooner or later you get tired of having so much company!

SCHULZ

※ SIGH ※

※ SIGH ※

AND THEY CALL **ME** PECULIAR!

SCHULZ

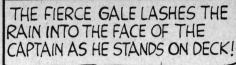

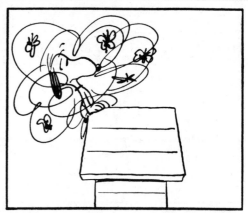

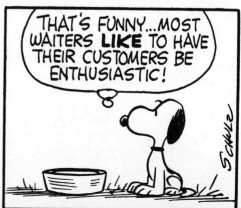

IT WAS NICE OF THEM TO ASK ME, BUT I JUST HAD TO SAY, "NO"

I SUPPOSE BECAUSE THEY USE MY PLACE FOR THEIR MEETINGS THEY FELT OBLIGATED TO ASK ME TO JOIN THEIR GROUP

I WONDER IF IT WOULD BE WRONG FOR ME TO LISTEN-IN ON ONE OF THEIR MEETINGS!?

THAT'S THE MOST FRIGHTENING THING I'VE EVER HEARD!

SEE THAT BIRD?

HE'S LISTENING... BIRDS CAN HEAR THE WORMS UNDER THE GROUND...

WHEN THEY HEAR A WORM, THEY REACH DOWN, AND PULL HIM OUT!

MUST BE PRETTY NOISY WORMS!

I JUST DON'T KNOW..

IT'S HARD FOR ME TO BELIEVE THAT BIRDS CAN HEAR WORMS UNDER THE GROUND..

IN FACT, THE THOUGHT THAT THE GROUND IS FULL OF WORMS SORT OF SHAKES ME UP...

IT MAKES MY FEET FEEL CREEPY!

THAT'S THE CLOSEST I'LL EVER COME TO KICKING A PIG!

PUNT

IF YOU'RE LOOKING FOR AN APPLE, I ATE THE LAST ONE..

BOY, IF YOU WEREN'T WEARING GLASSES, I'D SLUG YOU A GOOD ONE!

GLASSES ARE GOOD FOR YOUR EYES... THEY KEEP YOU FROM GETTING PUNCHED IN THEM!

THIS IS SERIOUS...HOW CAN YOU HELP SOMEONE WHO HAS BECOME A COMPULSIVE "WATER SPRINKLER-HEAD STANDER"?

IT'S VERY SIMPLE...JUST TURN OFF THE WATER!

THANK YOU... *SIGH*

LISTEN TO THIS, CHARLIE BROWN...

IT SAYS HERE THAT THERE ARE OVER SIX HUNDRED AND SEVENTY THOUSAND DIFFERENT KINDS OF INSECTS!

WOW!

TAKE COMFORT, LITTLE FELLOW... YOU ARE NOT ALONE!

TRAVEL MAKES A PERSON GROW...

NO ONE IS REALLY EDUCATED WHO HAS NOT SEEN NEW LANDS AND MET NEW PEOPLE...TRAVEL ADDS A TOUCH OF MATURITY...

I'LL GO ALONG WITH THAT.. I'M A GREAT BELIEVER IN TRAVEL..

AS LONG AS YOU DON'T GET OUT OF SIGHT OF THE SUPPER DISH!

I REALLY THINK YOU SHOULD BE ASHAMED OF YOURSELF!

NO DOG SHOULD EVER WASTE HIS TIME SLEEPING WHEN HE COULD BE OUT CHASING RABBITS!

I DON'T KNOW...SOME OF US ARE BORN DOGS, AND SOME OF US ARE BORN RABBITS...

WHEN THE CHIPS ARE DOWN, I'LL HAVE TO ADMIT THAT MY SYMPATHY LIES WITH THE RABBITS

ZOOM

WITH A LITTLE PRACTICE I BET I COULD GET THE SHOES, TOO!

PTUI!!

I WORRY ABOUT WHO'S GOING TO SEE HIM FIRST...A BIG-LEAGUE SCOUT OR THE HUMANE SOCIETY!

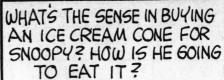

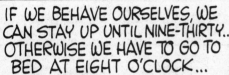

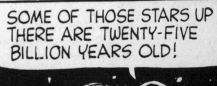

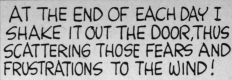

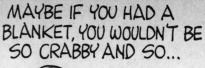

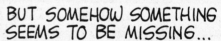

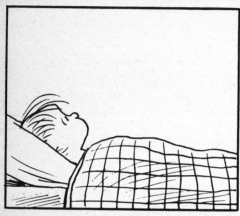

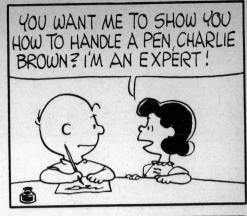

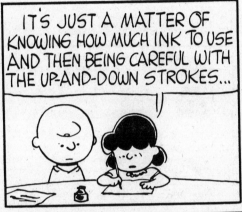

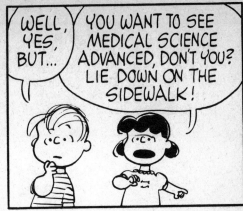

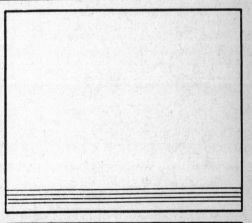

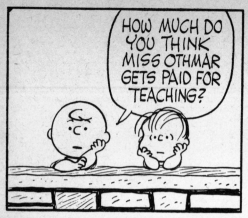

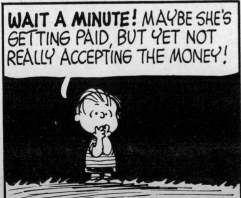

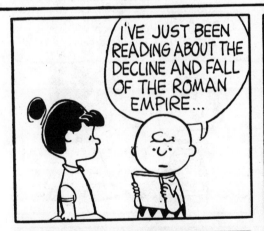

GOOD GRIEF! HERE COMES LUCY! I'M TRAPPED!

SHE SAID SHE'D THROW MY BLANKET IN THE TRASH BURNER THE NEXT TIME SHE SAW IT...

SCHULZ

DO YOU THINK I'M BEAUTIFUL, CHARLIE BROWN?

YOU DIDN'T ANSWER RIGHT AWAY! YOU HAD TO THINK ABOUT IT, DIDN'T YOU?

IF YOU HAD REALLY THOUGHT I WAS BEAUTIFUL, YOU WOULD HAVE SPOKEN RIGHT UP!!

I KNOW WHEN I'VE BEEN INSULTED!! I KNOW WHEN...

GOOD GRIEF!

SCHULZ

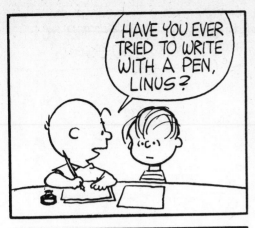

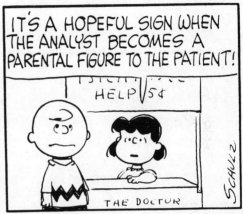

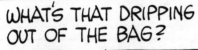

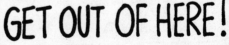

Panel 1: ALL RIGHT, SO I'M A BASEBALL SCOUT...WHAT DO I DO? / YOU GO, AND FIND OUT ALL YOU CAN ABOUT THEIR PITCHERS AND HITTERS..

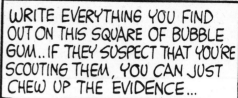

Panel 2: WRITE EVERYTHING YOU FIND OUT ON THIS SQUARE OF BUBBLE GUM..IF THEY SUSPECT THAT YOU'RE SCOUTING THEM, YOU CAN JUST CHEW UP THE EVIDENCE...

Panel 3: WELL, GOOD LUCK, OL' BUDDY... / THANK YOU, CHARLIE BROWN..

Panel 4: SOMEHOW I HAVE THE FEELING OF IMPENDING DOOM!

Panel 5: MAYBE I SHOULDN'T HAVE SENT LINUS OUT AS A BASEBALL SCOUT...

Panel 6: MAYBE HE'LL GET LOST..MAYBE THE OTHER TEAM WILL SEE WHAT HE'S DOING, AND BEAT HIM UP...

Panel 7: HEY, MANAGER, DO YOU THINK MY HAIR LOOKS ALL RIGHT THIS WAY, OR SHOULD I CHANGE IT? / NO, IT LOOKS FINE JUST THE WAY IT IS...

Panel 8: IT'S AWFUL TO HAVE TO BE THE ONE WHO MAKES ALL THE DECISIONS!

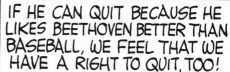

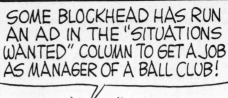